June 6, 2021

To: Quentin

From: Your CCC Family

Congratulations on
your graduation!

SCHOOL'S OUT
Life's On

WISDOM &
INSPIRATION
FOR
GRADUATES

Todd
Hafer

BroadStreet
PUBLISHING

BroadStreet Publishing Group, LLC
Racine, Wisconsin, USA
BroadStreetPublishing.com

School's Out, Life's On: WISDOM & INSPIRATION FOR GRADUATES

ISBN-13: 978-1-4245-5466-9 (hardcover)
ISBN-13: 978-1-4245-5471-3 (e-book)

Stock or custom editions of BroadStreet Publishing titles may be purchased in bulk for educational, business, ministry, fundraising, or sales promotional use. For information, please e-mail info@ broadstreetpublishing.com.

Cover design by Chris Garborg at garborgdesign.com
Interior by Katherine Lloyd at theDESKonline.com

Printed in China

17 18 19 20 21 5 4 3 2 1

Contents

School's Out ...
Life's On!

It's a big, exciting world out there, and every year thousands of fresh graduates are expected to jump in with both feet. If only diplomas and degrees came with complimentary life preservers.

The good news is that millions of people have navigated those waters before. They've made mistakes, enjoyed success, and learned to swim confidently in the great ocean called life. This book is filled with the wisdom, inspiration, and advice of the experienced. The experts. So, please, smartphones down. Eyes front. Pay attention as the ones who've been there teach some very important—and often entertaining—lessons on life.

Wise Words

From the class president to the class clown, everyone thinks, *I know a thing or two about life; I should be able to get by without a lot of outside assistance.*

But if we want to do more than merely "get by," it's wise to consider what others think, what others have learned. Here are some intriguing insights and quick bits of life-tested advice.

Anyone who STOPS LEARNING is OLD, whether at twenty or eighty. Anyone who KEEPS LEARNING stays YOUNG.

—Henry Ford, inventor
and automobile pioneer

A **SUCCESSFUL** man is the one who can lay a firm foundation with the **BRICKS** others have thrown at him.

—*David Brinkley, legendary TV news anchor*

For we are His creation, **CREATED** in Christ Jesus for good works, which God **PREPARED AHEAD** of time so that we should **WALK IN THEM.**

—*Saint Paul, missionary and church leader*
(Ephesians 2:19 HCSB)

The **SWEETEST THING** in all
my life has been the longing
to **FIND THE PLACE** where all
the **BEAUTY** came from.

—*C.S. Lewis, author and Christian apologist*

The highest REWARD
for your work is not
what you get for it,
but what you BECOME by it.

—*John Maxwell, best-selling author
and leadership trainer*

Love **NEVER GIVES UP**.
Love **CARES** for others
more than self.

—*Saint Paul, missionary and church leader*
(1 Corinthians 13:4 MSG)

It ain't over
till it's over.

*—Yogi Berra, Hall of Fame
baseball player and manager*

Take care! **PROTECT YOURSELF**
against the least bit
of **GREED**. Life is not defined
by what you have,
even when you have **A LOT**.

—*Jesus Christ*
(Luke 12:15 MSG)

It's what **YOU'VE LEARNED**
after you know it all
that **COUNTS**.

—*John Wooden,*
legendary basketball coach

Even in darkness
LIGHT DAWNS for the upright,
for those who are GRACIOUS
and COMPASSIONATE
and RIGHTEOUS.

—*Psalm 112:4*

How far you go in life depends on your **BEING TENDER** with the young, **COMPASSIONATE** with the aged, **SYMPATHETIC** with the striving, and **TOLERANT** of the weak and strong. Because someday in life, you will have **BEEN ALL** of these.

—*George Washington Carver, botanist and inventor*

Troubles are often the TOOLS
by which God FASHIONS US
for better things.

—Henry Ward Beecher, pastor and social reformer

GOD IS striding
ahead of you.
He's right there **WITH YOU**.
HE WON'T let you down;
HE WON'T leave you.
Don't be intimidated.
Don't worry.

—Moses, prophet, writer, and leader
(Deuteronomy 31:8 MSG)

I have learned that **SUCCESS** is to be **MEASURED** not so much by the position that one has reached in life … as by the obstacles which he has **OVERCOME** while **TRYING** to succeed.

—Booker T. Washington,
educator and US presidential advisor

God has a BEAUTIFUL way
of bringing GOOD VIBRATIONS
out of broken chords.

—*Chuck Swindoll,*
pastor, author, and educator

GOD WILL help
you **FLY OVER** what
you can't go through.

—*Woodrow Kroll, preacher and radio host*

It may be hard for an egg to TURN INTO A BIRD: it would be a jolly sight harder for it to learn to fly while remaining an egg. We are LIKE EGGS at present. And you cannot go on indefinitely being just an ordinary, decent egg. We must BE HATCHED or go bad.

—C. S. Lewis, author and Christian apologist

We know that in **ALL THINGS**
God works for **THE GOOD** of
those who **LOVE HIM**,
who have been **CALLED**
according to his **PURPOSE**.

—*Saint Paul, missionary and church leader*
(Romans 8:28)

It's a good thing to have
all **THE PROPS** pulled out from
under us occasionally.
It gives us some **SENSE** of
WHAT IS ROCK under our feet,
and what **IS SAND**.

—*Madeleine L'Engle, novelist*

Those who
DIVE IN the sea of affliction
bring up **RARE PEARLS**.

—Charles Spurgeon, British pastor and author

The Lord will
GUIDE YOU always;
he will **SATISFY** your needs in
a sun-scorched land and will
STRENGTHEN your frame.
You will be like a
well-watered garden,
like a spring whose
waters **NEVER FAIL**.

—*God, through the prophet Isaiah*
(Isaiah 58:11)

Worry is a cycle
of INEFFICIENT THOUGHTS
whirling around
a CENTER OF FEAR.

—*Corrie ten Boom,*
author and Holocaust survivor

LOVE will take you places
the mind can't see.
LOVE is what keeps me **ALIVE**.

—*Craig Sager, Hall of Fame broadcaster*

God does not give us
everything we want,
but he does FULFILL
his promises, LEADING US
along the best and
STRAIGHTEST PATH to himself.

—Dietrich Bonhoeffer,
German pastor and theologian

Every day we are CALLED
to do small things
with GREAT LOVE.

—Mother Teresa,
missionary and Nobel Peace Prize winner

LOVE is the
greatest **BEAUTIFIER**
in the universe.

—May Christie, writer

What COUNTS is
not necessarily the size
of the dog in the fight,
but the size of THE
FIGHT in the dog.

—Dwight D. Eisenhower,
five-star general and US president

A quiet conscience sleeps in thunder.

—*English proverb*

There is **PROFIT** in all **HARD WORK**, but endless talk leads only to poverty.

—*King Solomon of Israel*
(Proverbs 14:23 HCSB)

Character is power.

—Booker T. Washington,
educator and US presidential advisor

Trials **TEACH US** what we are;
they **DIG UP** the soil and let us
see what we **ARE MADE OF**.

*—Charles Spurgeon, author, pastor,
and philanthropist*

BEWARE in your prayers, above everything else, of **LIMITING GOD**, not only by unbelief, but by fancying that **YOU KNOW** what he can do.

—*Andrew Murray, minister and author*

The two most
powerful warriors
are **PATIENCE** and **TIME**.

—*Leo Tolstoy, author and leader*

The **IMPORTANT THING** is not to stop questioning. **CURIOSITY** has its own reason for existence.

—*Albert Einstein, author and physicist*

All the darkness in the world
CANNOT EXTINGUISH the
LIGHT of a single candle.

—*Saint Francis of Assisi,*
soldier and spiritual leader

If [your gift] is to encourage,
then **GIVE ENCOURAGEMENT**;
if it is giving,
then **GIVE GENEROUSLY**.

—*Saint Paul, missionary and church leader*
(Romans 12:8)

We are what we
repeatedly do.
EXCELLENCE, then, is not
an act but **A HABIT.**

—*Aristotle, philosopher, scientist,
and teacher*

OPPORTUNITY is missed
by most people because
it is dressed in overalls
and looks like **WORK**.

—*Thomas Edison, inventor and businessman*

SUCCESS is a lousy teacher.
It **SEDUCES** smart people into
thinking they **CAN'T LOSE**.

—*Bill Gates,*
entrepreneur and philanthropist

Hard **WORK SPOTLIGHTS**
the **CHARACTER** of people:
Some turn up their sleeves,
some turn up their noses,
and some don't
TURN UP at all.

—*Sam Ewing, professional baseball player
and college professor*

Words can never
adequately convey the
incredible IMPACT of our
ATTITUDES toward life.
The longer I live, the more
convinced I become that life
is 10 percent WHAT HAPPENS
to us and 90 percent
how WE RESPOND to it.

—*Chuck Swindoll, pastor, author,*
and educator

GREATNESS lies not
in being strong, but in
the right **USE OF STRENGTH**.

—*Henry Ward Beecher,*
pastor and social reformer

WELL DONE is better
than **WELL SAID**.

—*Benjamin Franklin,*
inventor and US founding father

We may ENCOUNTER many DEFEATS, but we must not be DEFEATED.

—*Maya Angelou, writer and civil-rights activist*

Mountaintops are for
views and inspiration,
but **FRUIT** is **GROWN**
in the **VALLEYS**.

—Billy Graham,
pastor, evangelist, and author

SUCCESS is going from failure
to failure **WITHOUT LOSING**
your **ENTHUSIASM**.

—*Abraham Lincoln,*
lawyer and US president

If you do not **HOPE**,
you will not **FIND** what is
BEYOND your hopes.

—*Saint Clement of Alexandria,
teacher and theologian*

For I know THE PLANS
I have for you,
plans to PROSPER you
and not to harm you,
plans to GIVE YOU
hope and A FUTURE.

—*God, through the prophet Jeremiah*
(Jeremiah 29:11)

When you can do the
COMMON THINGS of life in
an UNCOMMON WAY,
you will command the
ATTENTION of the world.

—George Washington Carver,
botanist and inventor

He is **RICHEST**
who is **CONTENT** with
the **LEAST.**

—*Socrates, philosopher and teacher*

No one can make you
FEEL INFERIOR without
your **CONSENT**.

—*Eleanor Roosevelt,*
diplomat and humanitarian

It's not how much WE HAVE,
but how much WE ENJOY,
that makes HAPPINESS.

—*Charles Spurgeon, British pastor and author*

I am a slow walker,
but I never walk backward.

—*Abraham Lincoln,*
lawyer and US president

GENIUS is 99 percent
perspiration
and 1 percent **INSPIRATION**.

—*Thomas Edison, inventor and businessman*

THINKING is the **HARDEST WORK** there is, which is probably the reason so few people **ENGAGE IN IT.**

—Henry Ford, inventor and automobile pioneer

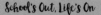

The **ONLY ONE** who never makes **MISTAKES** is the one who never **DOES ANYTHING.**

—*Theodore Roosevelt, US president, soldier, and environmentalist*

When **FAITH** is small
and **HOPE** doubts,
LOVE conquers.

—*Thelma Wells, author and speaker*

We can never know
WHO WE ARE until we
know at least
something of WHAT GOD IS.

—*A. W. Tozer, pastor and author*

PERSPECTIVE is everything when you are **EXPERIENCING** the **CHALLENGES** of life.

—*Joni Eareckson Tada,*
artist, singer, and author

Fame is a vapor,
popularity an accident,
riches take wing,
and only **CHARACTER ENDURES**.

—*Horace Greeley, newspaper pioneer
and social reformer*

LOVE is the most **IMPORTANT** thing in the world, but baseball is pretty **GOOD TOO**.

—*Yogi Berra, Hall of Fame baseball player and manager*

It is the NEGLECT of
timely repair that makes
REBUILDING necessary.

—*Richard Whatley, economist and theologian*

In this world
it is not what we TAKE UP,
but what we GIVE UP,
that makes us RICH.

—Henry Ward Beecher,
pastor and social reformer

DARE to **DISCOVER** what you believe in. Then have the **COURAGE** to believe in what you have **DISCOVERED**.

—Todd Hafer, author

It's kind of FUN to do
the IMPOSSIBLE.

—*Walt Disney,*
entrepreneur and filmmaker

No **ADVICE** on success

WORKS

unless you **DO.**

—*John Maxwell, best-selling author
and leadership trainer*

A **GENEROUS** person
will be **BLESSED**.

—*King Solomon of Israel*
(Proverbs 22:9 HCSB)

HOPE is the power
of being **CHEERFUL** in
CIRCUMSTANCES which we
know to be desperate.

—*G. K. Chesterton, author,
philosopher and theologian*

The place God CALLS YOU TO
is the place where your
DEEP GLADNESS and the world's
great hunger MEET.

—*Frederick Buechner,*
pastor, theologian, and author

Signs You're Studying Too Hard

1. You find yourself highlighting portions of a restaurant menu.

2. You keep entering your student ID into your microwave oven.

3. Your love letters contain bullet points and footnotes.

4. When you talk in your sleep, you recite the periodic table of the elements.

5. The school library just named a study carrel after YOU.

Sound Advice

Want to get ahead in life? Then follow the lead of others who have been there, tried it, and learned the simple secrets of success. This section gives extra credit to those who truly believe what they are talking about—believe it strongly enough to follow their own advice.

Let **LOVE** and **FAITHFULNESS**
never leave you;
BIND THEM around
your neck, **WRITE THEM** on
the tablet of your heart.
Then you will **WIN FAVOR** and
a **GOOD NAME** in the sight
of God and man.

—*King Solomon of Israel*
(Proverbs 3:3–4)

If you **CAN'T** do it
with feeling,
DON'T.

—*Patsy Cline,*
legendary country singer/songwriter

God DESIGNS US to
want to do what we are
MOST CAPABLE of doing.
Because of this, when we do
things that are making
AN IMPACT, something
RESONATES within us.

—*John Maxwell, best-selling author
and leadership trainer*

Don't be afraid to **BE AFRAID**.
We cannot **CONQUER** fear
without **ACKNOWLEDGING**
it first. If we had no fears,
we wouldn't know
what **COURAGE IS**.

—*Todd Hafer, author*

You may have to **FIGHT A BATTLE** more than once to **WIN IT.**

—Margaret Thatcher,
Britain's first female prime minister

Even if you're on the **RIGHT TRACK**, you'll get run over if you just **SIT THERE**.

—*Will Rogers, humorist and writer*

Always **DO RIGHT**.
This will **GRATIFY SOME** people
and **ASTONISH** the rest.

—*Mark Twain, author and speaker*

LAZY hands
make for POVERTY,
but DILIGENT hands
bring WEALTH.

—*King Solomon of Israel*
(Proverbs 10:4)

First **KEEP PEACE**
within yourself,
then you can also
BRING PEACE
to others.

—*Thomas à Kempis, priest and writer*

Don't ever take
a fence down
until you **KNOW WHY**
it was put up.

—*Robert Frost, US poet laureate*

God has given us
two hands—one to
RECEIVE WITH and the other
to **GIVE WITH**. We are not
cisterns made for hoarding;
we are **CHANNELS**
made **FOR SHARING**.

—Billy Graham, author, evangelist,
and pastor

I'm **ABSOLUTELY CONVINCED**
that nothing—**NOTHING** living
or dead, angelic or demonic,
today or tomorrow,
high or low, thinkable or
unthinkable—absolutely
NOTHING can get between
us and **GOD'S LOVE** because
of the way that Jesus our
Master **HAS EMBRACED US**.

—*Saint Paul, missionary and church leader*
(Romans 8:39 MSG)

It is in **GIVING** oneself
that one **RECEIVES**.

—*Saint Francis of Assisi,
soldier and spiritual leader*

You are **NOT THE SUM**
of your weaknesses
and failures; you are
THE SUM of the Father's
love for you and your real
capacity to **BECOME**
the **IMAGE OF HIS SON**.

—*Pope John Paul II*

I am sure of this,
that He who started
a **GOOD WORK** in you will
carry it on **TO COMPLETION**
until the day of Christ Jesus.

—*Saint Paul, missionary and church leader*
(Philippians 1:6 HCSB)

My SUCCESSES
have INSPIRED me,
but my failures have
made me STRONGER.

—*Todd Hafer, author*

Concentrate on counting
YOUR BLESSINGS and
you'll have little time
to count **ANYTHING ELSE.**

—*Woodrow Kroll, preacher and radio host*

Be kind and COMPASSIONATE
to one another,
FORGIVING each other,
just as in Christ
God FORGAVE you.

—*Saint Paul, missionary and church leader*
(Ephesians 4:32)

Remember not only
to **SAY** the right thing
at the right place, but to
LEAVE UNSAID the wrong thing
at the tempting moment.

—*Benjamin Franklin, inventor
and US founding father*

Dreams don't work—
unless you do.

—*John Maxwell, best-selling author
and leadership trainer*

Dream
no small dream.

—Victor Hugo, poet and novelist

To be CLEVER ENOUGH
to get all of the money,
one must be
STUPID ENOUGH to want it.

—*G. K. Chesterton, author,*
philosopher, and theologian

PLAN ahead.
It wasn't raining when
Noah **BUILT** the ark.

—*Cardinal Richard Cushing*

SERVE one another
humbly **IN LOVE**.

—*Saint Paul, missionary and church leader*
(Galatians 5:13)

There's a difference
between **FOLLOWING JESUS** …
and **FOLLOWING JESUS**
on Facebook,
Twitter, and Instagram.

—*Jedd Hafer, author and speaker*

Where our **WORK IS**,
there let our **JOY BE**.

—*Tertullian,*
author and theologian

Life is either **A DARING ADVENTURE** or nothing.

—*Helen Keller,*
author and speaker

MONEY never
made anyone **RICH**.

—*Seneca the Younger,
philosopher and statesman*

FRIENDSHIP is one of the **SWEETEST JOYS** of life. Many might have failed beneath the bitterness of their trial, had they not **FOUND A FRIEND.**

—*Charles Spurgeon, author, pastor, and philanthropist*

HUMILITY is not thinking
less of yourself;
it is thinking
of YOURSELF LESS.

—*Rick Warren, author and pastor*

Do or do not.
There is **NO TRY**.

—*Yoda, wise Jedi Master*

NEVER FORGET that only dead fish always **SWIM** with the stream.

—*Malcolm Muggeridge,*
soldier, spy, and author

YESTERDAY is a
cancelled check;
TOMORROW is
a promissory note.
TODAY is the only
cash you have,
so **SPEND** it wisely.

—*Kay Lyons, writer*

He is no fool who
GIVES what he
cannot keep **TO GAIN**
that which he **CANNOT LOSE.**

—Jim Elliot, missionary

You should use
whatever GIFT you have
received to SERVE OTHERS,
as faithful stewards
of GOD'S GRACE in
its various forms.

—*Saint Peter, missionary and church leader*
(1 Peter 4:10)

TAKE CHARGE of
your thoughts.
You can do what you
WILL WITH THEM.

—*Plato, philosopher and educator*

Some people DRINK at
the fountain of knowledge.
Others JUST GARGLE.

—*American proverb*

Be sure to fear the Lord
and **SERVE HIM** faithfully
with all your heart;
CONSIDER what great things
he has done **FOR YOU**.

—*Samuel, prophet and leader*
(1 Samuel 12:24)

I bring you THE GIFT of these four words:

I BELIEVE IN YOU.

—Blaise Pascal, mathematician, inventor, philosopher, and writer

Those who say it cannot be done should **NOT INTERRUPT** the person doing it.

—*Chinese proverb*

TODAY is non-returnable.

Make it **UNFORGETTABLE**.

—*Barbara Loots, writer*

HARD WORK always pays off;
mere talk puts
no bread **ON THE TABLE.**

—*King Solomon of Israel*
(Proverbs 14:23 MSG)

My father always told me, "Find a JOB YOU LOVE and you'll never have to WORK A DAY in your life."

—*Jim Fox, hockey player and sportscaster*

Please **LIVE** a good life.
I don't want to **HAVE TO LIE**
at your funeral.

—*Jerry Springston, pastor*

NOT-So-Sound Advice

Every year, people hand out graduation advice like it's Halloween candy. But how much of this advice truly *works*? In this section, recent (and not-so-recent) graduates share advice that *sounded good* at the time, but did not make the grade in the real world.

"Don't worry about grades. Employers don't care about your GPA."

In high school and college, many of my peers—and a few teachers—told me, "Don't stress about grades. Employers don't really care about them. No one even looks at GPAs or transcripts anymore." I studied hard anyway. After college, during my first job interview, my boss-to-be told me he was impressed with my GPA. He said, "I make it a habit to hire honor students whenever I can."

Today, I am a manager, and I've never gone wrong by hiring excellent students. A candidate's GPA is not the only factor, but there is just something about people who are willing to put in the time and effort to achieve excellence—in the classroom and on the job.

—*Sherry, age 35*

> *"Don't start college until you know exactly what you're going to major in."*

Did you know that most people change jobs at least six times in their lifetime? I learned this during my freshman year of college. Since my major was "undeclared" at the time, I found the statistic comforting. After I graduated from high school, many of my relatives warned me that I was wasting my money by heading off to college without knowing my ultimate field of study.

This worried me. But then I had a chance conversation with the disc jockey at my college town's major radio station. He revealed that he began college as a forestry major, because he liked the idea of working outdoors. However, at a college radio station, he fell in love with broadcast journalism. He told me he knew dozens of fellow students who changed their majors—some of them multiple times.

"Don't worry about declaring a major as a frosh, or even a sophomore," he told me. "That major will probably change anyway. Just learn—and learn how to learn!"

What a relief! I didn't have to define the rest of my working life during my first college semester. So I focused on tackling my required courses. Eventually, I chose a major in business—only to change to applied math two semesters later. When I settled on this major, I was grateful to have so much of my required coursework out of the way. I ended up saving myself at least a semester's worth of time and expense. And I was able to enter the job market much sooner.

—*Scott, age 28*

The Lucky 7

SEVEN TIPS FOR A SUCCESSFUL JOB OR SCHOLARSHIP INTERVIEW

1. Be completely honest.

2. Dress appropriately.

3. Be positive, but sincere.

4. Listen as much as you talk.

5. Don't be afraid to ask questions and seek clarification.

6. Be respectful of the interviewer's time—and feelings.

7. Be sure to follow up with a thank-you note. (Set yourself apart by handwriting your thank-you.)

"College is a great place to find a spouse."

Before I left home for college, my mom urged me, "We're sending you to a good Christian school; find a good Christian man there!"

I did find a good man. However, I quit school to get married, establish a home, and start a family.

Don't get me wrong: I do not regret getting married, but I did feel incomplete for years and years. Finally, after two full decades, I returned to college and finished my degree. Then I got a great job. Then I started my own company. Then I hired my husband to help with the finances and other business details!

Sure, there's nothing wrong with keeping your eyes open for an intriguing fellow college student. But college is not a dating service. Engagement 101 is not a core course. So don't feel bad if you don't meet "the one" before you graduate. Don't force it.

Remember that people change so much between ages eighteen and twenty-two. Your "perfect someone" at eighteen will differ from that

A Road Map to Achievement

Believe while others doubt.

Plan while others vegetate.

Study while others goof off.

Decide while others delay.

Take responsibility while others make excuses.

Begin while others procrastinate.

Work while others wish.

Save while others spend.

Listen while others pontificate.

Smile while others pout.

Commend while others criticize.

Persist while others quit.

of age twenty-two or twenty-three. Besides, when you do meet interesting students, you don't want to have that odor of desperation oozing from your pores.

In life, your goal should be to marry your *ideal* mate, not necessarily your classmate. Hey, if you end up meeting the perfect person at school … cool. If not, settle for a good education and move on to enter that even bigger pool of romance candidates known as the Big Wide World.

—*Rachel, age 50*

> "There's no way to avoid the Freshman 15, so you might as well accept the extra weight."

Ah, the Freshman 15. That extra poundage we're all sure to gain as we switch from home cooking to Taco Bell, Mickey D's, and the overindulgence afforded by all-you-can-eat cafeteria food. And let's not forget the late-night study sessions, complete with piles of buttery popcorn and the economy-sized bag of chips.

The food situation at my college—coupled with the fact that PE was purely optional—left me finishing my frosh year seventeen pounds heavier than when I began. (Yeah, I opted for no PE. No exercise of any kind, really.)

No sweat, I consoled myself. *I can burn off the unwanted pounds during the summer.*

And I did. Sort of. A summer job waiting tables—combined with a return to my workout routine—allowed me to drop twelve of my Freshman 17. The problem was that my sophomore year saw me gain the Sophomore 16. The result: I faced the summer between my soph and junior years a full twenty-one pounds heavier than when I enrolled. Curse you, math! And curse you, lack of discipline!

I told myself that drastic measures were in order. But I ended up not having to resort to lipo or some kind or fitness boot camp. During my junior year, I exercised at least five times a week. Even if it was just taking a long walk. And I also exercised discipline in what I ate: My school offered chocolate pudding every day; I did not have to eat it every day. Just sayin'.

I found that the school cafeteria actually provided some healthful choices—if I was willing to look for them, rather than head for the familiar nacho bar for every lunch and dinner. One of my secrets was to drink a large glass of water and eat a piece of dry multigrain toast, or toast with sugar-free jam, at every meal. This move helped me fill up without adding tons of calories and fat.

Also, I dug my tennis racket out of the closet and started playing three or four times a week with girls from my dorm. In high school, I thought tennis was a sport for geeky girls. But there was nothing geeky about the way the weight dropped off—and my arms and legs began to exhibit signs of actual muscle tone. (Also not geeky: the hot guys who often occupied the surrounding courts!)

Here's a happy truth: You are not doomed to the Freshman 15 simply because Mom and Dad are not there to make sure you eat right and get your exercise. With a little self-discipline, those added college pounds can be toast.

—*Sarah, age 28*

Ten Things to Make at Work—Besides Money

1. Time
2. Merry
3. Do
4. Up
5. Sense
6. Peace
7. Room
8. Waves
9. Amends
10. Believe

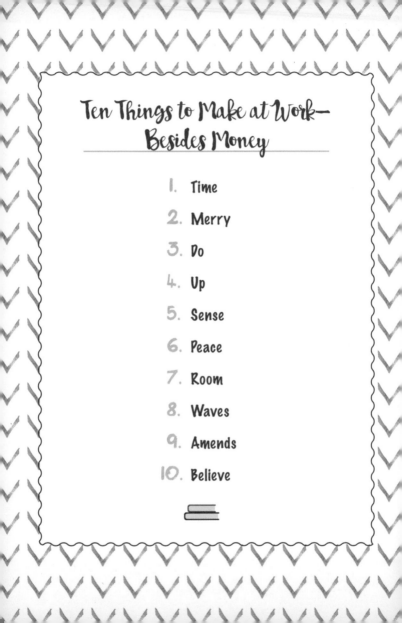

"In choosing a career, go where the money is."

Money for money's sake creates many frustrated people. I am one of them. During college, my friends bragged about how much they would make once they hit the job market. They said things like, "I'm not going to even consider a job unless it pays eighty thousand a year!"

I got caught up in the competition and ended up pursing a lucrative career. I really wanted to open my own sporting goods store, but I got laughed out of the room the first time I mentioned this dream to my college buddies.

So, I went into another field, and I have made good money. Really good money. But I have also worked insane hours. And I've been laid off twice—largely because I am in a cutthroat business. (I have to admit, though, that it's hard to strive for excellence at a job I often despise. I'm sure my bosses are clued in to this.)

I don't like "old adages," but, wow, "Money can't buy happiness"—that is as true as the sun in

the sky. Sure, I can afford a lot of expensive "toys," but the problem with toys is that you outgrow them pretty quickly. (Anyone want to buy a slightly used Jet Ski?)

After all is said and done, if your career isn't linked to your life's passion, you're going to feel empty, stressed, and unfulfilled. A lawyer friend of mine recently told me that he would have rather worked with his hands—doing woodworking or something—because that's what he loves to do.

Here's my advice: Don't search for money. Money will find you when you are doing what you love. God will provide. So follow your passion.

—Stephen, age 40

The Cans and Cannots of Money

Money can buy you

a bed, but not sleep;

books, but not brains;

food, but not appetite;

fitness equipment, but not fitness itself;

surface beauty, but not inner beauty;

a house, but not a home;

medicine, but not health;

amusement, but not happiness;

watches and clocks, but not time.

"Whatever you do, get out of this place."

There's nothing wrong with looking at education options beyond your hometown. But remember that a lot of people do better in life with a good support system around them. Family, friends, job, church, and mentors—these are often vital to helping a person thrive.

It's tough to re-create that stable and well-constructed network in a new place somewhere across the country. It takes a lot of time—if it happens at all.

If you have a legitimate plan to attend school and/or pursue opportunities in a new, faraway place, that's great. But I hope and pray that you will have support from across the miles as you build a great new support network. Just do not do what I did: I picked the most distant university I could find—both as an escape from my small hometown, and as a badge of courage. My classmates thought I was bold and adventurous to move so far away from home, to a school and a town where I knew not a single soul.

I quickly plunged into misery. I ended up staying at college for my freshman year, but only because I was too embarrassed to admit I had made a huge mistake.

Here is what I wish I had known then: Just because a place is "somewhere else" doesn't mean it's better. Now, I'm not saying a person is usually better off living with parents and attending a college close to home. But don't assume that "escaping" for its own sake is the answer. Especially if what you are escaping is actually pretty good.

People who insist that grads must get out of Dodge (or wherever) often resent where they are in life. And that resentment usually has little to do with geographic location. If, after graduation, you find a great situation close to home, don't be embarrassed that you didn't "get out."

Maybe you're already in the perfect place for you. Maybe you don't have anything to escape after all.

—*Ron, age 27*

> "Partying is part of the college experience. Don't be afraid to get a little crazy."

Reality check: The problem with sowing your wild oats is that, just as the Bible says, you reap what you sow. In other words, the decisions you make now affect the future—sometimes in drastic ways. As I write this short essay, I am still saddened by the story of a promising young college student who literally drank herself to death at a college party in my Colorado town. One reckless choice in college can lead to a lifetime of hardship and regret. Or, to no lifetime at all.

You don't have to live a boring lifestyle in college, but you should be smart about it. And not just for your own sake. Consider the people who care about you. Consider the people you influence. Please treat your life like the valuable gift it is. It takes only one instance of living dangerously with drugs, alcohol, or sex to throw a life off course …. or destroy it. There is no such thing as a *minor* lapse of integrity.

All through my college years, I watched people around me make bad choices, careless choices. They paid dearly for it. So sow wisely, not wildly.

—Jay, age 34

> "Don't be in a hurry to start college;
> take a couple years off
> to 'discover yourself.'"

Here's what I discovered after I delayed furthering my education to "discover myself": I wasted two whole years of my life—years I can never get back. And, at the end of my Discovery Period, I was no closer to being who, what, or where I wanted to be than on the day I walked across a squeaky high school stage to receive my diploma.

Believe this: Post-high school life isn't really about discovering who you are. It's about *becoming* who you want to be. And the "becoming process" takes work, discipline, and active thinking. My grandpa used to say, "If you aim at nothing, you're sure to hit it."

He was right. I spent two years drifting. I strived for nothing. I planned for nothing. I worked toward nothing. What did I have to show for it?

Nothing.

Like a lot of my friends, I used the "taking

time to find myself" line as an excuse to my parents, teachers, church youth leader, and other concerned adults. In reality, I was nervous about starting college. And, though it hurts to admit it, I was lazy. I didn't want to go to class and study anymore.

My friends and I kept saying, "We just aren't ready for college yet. Why tackle something you aren't ready for?"

Here's why: Delaying college for months—or even years—did not make any of us more ready. Whatever you are doing in life right now is preparing you for what you are going to do in the future. So, we were all preparing ourselves to take even more time off to find ourselves! In reality, the only finding this approach leads to is finding oneself without skills, without an education, and without a job. Oh yeah, and without a life.

My advice to you? If you want to find yourself, find yourself doing something meaningful to prepare for the rest of your life.

—Jen, age 23

It's OK to Change Careers

Consider the career paths of the following:

Gerald R. Ford: model turned US president

Dean Martin: steel worker turned entertainer

Golda Meir: school teacher turned Israeli prime minister

Howard Cosell: attorney turned broadcaster

Tim Green: NFL lineman turned novelist and attorney

John Grisham: lawyer turned best-selling author

Babe Ruth: bartender turned baseball player

Boris Karloff: Realtor turned horror-flick actor

Clark Gable: lumberjack turned actor

Paul Gaugin: stockbroker turned artist

Steve Martin: magician turned comedian and musician

Albert Einstein: patent-office clerk turned physicist

Patrick Cummins: barista turned mixed martial arts fighter

Mike Reid: professionasl football player turned country music star

Vitali Klitschko: professionasl boxer turned Ukrainian political leader

Ina Garten: nuclear policy analyst turned cookbook author and Food Network host

Margaret Thatcher: chemist turned British prime minister

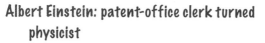

A Final Thought

WHAT I'VE LEARNED ABOUT LEARNING

• • •

By Lauren Benson

Creative Director - Editorial for Hallmark

When a friend of mine graduated a year ahead of me, his dad told him, "Up to this point, you've been learning for other people. From this point forward, everything you learn is for yourself."

This comment sparked several questions for me: How do I learn for myself? How is that different from learning for other people? What do I need to learn for myself? What will I want to learn after I have graduated—when the learning is optional, not for an assignment? For that matter, have I been learning "for myself" at all so far?

I still ponder these questions. In fact, my friend's father's statement is like an intellectual trust fund that I'll spend a lifetime drawing from. It's that self-sustaining, that permanent, and that mysterious. I should really send that dad a thank-you note for the gift he unwittingly gave me. Even if it was a present that hurt.

You see, at the time, I was a straight-A student,

but I got this uneasy, gnawing feeling that I had just failed an assignment. It took me back to sixth grade, and an algebra quiz that yielded my worst grade ever: a D-minus. Reading that grade, I was slightly baffled as to where things had gone so wrong.

As it turned out, I had forgotten about the properties of negative numbers when I did my multiplying and dividing. I boldly calculated and computed my problem set, breezed through the simple exercises, and then turned in my quiz—without even a second glance at the page.

I missed almost half the questions.

Similarly, there were times in college when I huffed and puffed through assignments, plugged through research papers and essays, and nodded through lectures—all without so much as glancing up from my notes and trying to get a sense of the big picture. I missed so much as a result.

Moreover, I looked at life the way I looked at an essay or some other college assignment. It seemed like something I could breeze through. Just give me a little bit of luck and some well-timed inspiration.

Let me tell you—that is not the way I look at life now. Sure, I still hope for inspiration. And I'm wide open to whatever heavenly blessings might drop into my lap. But I know that I will miss out on true success if I don't invest myself fully in life.

Today, I have so many doors open to me. I am free from the constraints of college life: tests, assignments, group projects, social pressures, and the bureaucracy endemic to higher education.

Fortunately, my perspective has changed since college. Yes, I am certainly more intellectually prepared for life in the "real world" than I was as a student. Some early success at my job can attest to that. The changes that I'm most pleased with, though, are deeper.

I am learning that great people are not distinguished by age, but rather by their firm resolve and pure intent. I am learning to be curious rather than afraid. I am looking at my work "assignments" as opportunities to discover and interpret for myself a fascinating, multifaceted, and perpetually surprising world.

Of course, there have been days when I'd

rather call in sick and catch up on my sleep. But most of the time I can't wait to get to work. To create, to interact, and to learn from the amazing people who surround me at Hallmark.

I am thankful to God that there is—and always will be—more than enough to discover.

Lauren Benson, *a graduate of St. Olaf College in Northfield, Minnesota, was recently promoted to the position of Creative Director–Editorial at Hallmark Cards, Inc.*

May you be blessed
by the LORD,
the Maker of
heaven and earth.

—*Psalm 115:15*

About the Author

Todd Hafer, a graduate of Buffalo High School (in Buffalo, Wyoming) and the University of Colorado, has written more than sixty books. His "day job" is senior acquisitions editor at Harvest House Publishers. He lives with his family in Eugene, Oregon.